# WASHINGTON
# REDSKINS

by Ryan Basen

Published by ABDO Publishing Company, 8000 West 78th Street, Edina, Minnesota 55439. Copyright © 2011 by Abdo Consulting Group, Inc. International copyrights reserved in all countries. No part of this book may be reproduced in any form without written permission from the publisher. SportsZone™ is a trademark and logo of ABDO Publishing Company.

Printed in the United States of America,
North Mankato, Minnesota
062010
092010

THIS BOOK CONTAINS AT LEAST 10% RECYCLED MATERIALS.

Editor: Matt Tustison
Copy Editor: Nicholas Cafarelli
Interior Design and Production: Christa Schneider
Cover Design: Craig Hinton

**Photo Credits:** LM Otero/AP Images, cover; AP Images, title page, 4, 7, 10, 14, 18, 22, 31, 42, 43 (top); ER/AP Images, 9; File/AP Images, 13; NFL Photos/AP Images, 16, 26, 35; Harvey Georges/AP Images, 21; CWH/AP Images, 25; Jim Mone/AP Images, 28; Elise Amendola/AP Images, 33, 43 (middle); Paul Abell/AP Images, 36; Evan Vucci, File/AP Images, 39; Evan Vucci/AP Images, 41, 43 (bottom); David Stluka/AP Images, 44; David Drapkin/AP Images, 47

**Library of Congress Cataloging-in-Publication Data**
Basen, Ryan.
  Washington Redskins / Ryan Basen.
      p. cm. — (Inside the NFL)
  Includes index.
  ISBN 978-1-61714-032-7
  1.  Washington Redskins (Football team)—History—Juvenile literature.  I. Title.
  GV956.W3B34 2010
  796.332'6409753—dc22
                                        2010017874

# TABLE OF CONTENTS

# CHAPTER 1

# RETURN TO GLORY

**J**oe Gibbs had a tough decision to make. The Washington Redskins faced a fourth down at the Miami Dolphins' 43-yard line early in the fourth quarter of Super Bowl XVII. Washington trailed 17–13. The Redskins needed less than a yard for the first down.

Gibbs, Washington's coach, decided to go for the first down. The Redskins called "70 chip." It was designed for running back John Riggins to take the handoff and run left. It would go down as one of the most dramatic plays in Redskins history.

Super Bowl XVII was held on January 30, 1983, at the Rose Bowl in Pasadena, California. It was the second Super Bowl in which the Redskins had played. The first came after the 1972 season. In January 1983, Gibbs was completing his second season as Redskins coach. He would win three Super Bowls with Washington and lead the Redskins to a fourth during his first stint as the team's coach, from 1981 to 1992.

THE REDSKINS' JOHN RIGGINS BREAKS AWAY FROM THE DOLPHINS' DON MCNEAL ON HIS WAY TO A 43-YARD TOUCHDOWN RUN IN SUPER BOWL XVII.

# JOE GIBBS

Joe Gibbs coached the Redskins from 1981 to 1992 and again from 2004 to 2007. During his first stint, Gibbs guided Washington to three NFL titles, four NFC titles, five NFC East titles, and eight playoff berths. He led the Redskins to two playoff berths in his second stint.

Overall, Gibbs had a record of 171–101, including 17–7 in the postseason. He was inducted into the Pro Football Hall of Fame in 1996.

Gibbs began his NFL coaching career as an assistant with the St. Louis Cardinals in 1973. He later was an assistant with the Tampa Bay Buccaneers and the San Diego Chargers before he joined the Redskins.

Gibbs retired in 1993 to run a National Association for Stock Car Auto Racing (NASCAR) team. But he returned to the Redskins in 2004. He retired again after the 2007 season, at age 67.

But as of January 1983, the Redskins had not yet won a Super Bowl. In fact, Washington had not won a National Football League (NFL) championship since 1942. The team's fans were desperate for one. The 1982 season was Washington's best in a decade. The Redskins went 8–1 in a strike-shortened year. They then won three straight National Football Conference (NFC) playoff games to get to Super Bowl XVII.

Washington fell behind Miami early. The Dolphins were led by a great defense and coach Don Shula. He had already won two Super Bowls and was coaching in his fifth. It appeared that the experienced Shula was going to hold off Gibbs.

Only 10 minutes remained in the game as Washington

WASHINGTON'S JOE THEISMANN PREPARES TO THROW DURING SUPER BOWL XVII. THEISMANN PASSED FOR TWO TOUCHDOWNS AGAINST MIAMI.

faced the key fourth-down play. Quarterback Joe Theismann took the snap and handed the ball to Riggins. He ran left and saw a defender closing quickly at the line of scrimmage. It was Don McNeal. The cornerback was unblocked and had a free

### DID YOU KNOW?

The Redskins dominated Super Bowl XVII's second half. Washington's defense held Miami to two first downs and 34 yards of offense, including no passing yards. The offense scored 17 straight points. For the game, the Redskins outgained the Dolphins 400–176 and tallied 24 first downs to just nine for Miami.

shot at Riggins. He hit Riggins around the waist before the first-down marker.

Few cornerbacks could bring down the 6-foot-2, 240-pound Riggins. He continued churning his feet as McNeal hit him. The cornerback then slid down Riggins' legs and fell to the ground. Riggins accelerated past the first-down marker, leaving McNeal behind. No other Miami players stood in his way. Not only would Riggins get the first down. He was going to score.

As Riggins raced down the sideline into the end zone, anyone listening to the Redskins' radio broadcast heard the call by play-by-play man Frank Herzog: "He's gone! He's gone! Touchdown, Washington Redskins!"

Washington had the lead for the first time in the game. The Redskins' defense then stuffed the Dolphins, and the offense embarked on another big drive. When Theismann tossed a short touchdown pass to Charlie Brown with just less than two minutes to play, Washington went ahead 27–17. That would be the final score.

As Theismann walked off the field, he held the ball high with one hand. With his other

## JOHN RIGGINS

*John Riggins played running back for the Redskins from 1976 to 1979 and 1981 to 1985. He sat out the 1980 season because of a contract dispute. Riggins rushed for 166 yards and a touchdown in the Super Bowl XVII win. The 166 yards were a Super Bowl record at the time. Through 2009, Riggins was the Redskins' all-time leading rusher with 7,472 yards. Nicknamed "The Diesel," he was inducted into the Pro Football Hall of Fame in 1992. Riggins was known as a workhorse back who gained the tough yards inside and near the goal line. He played college football at the University of Kansas. After playing five seasons with the New York Jets, he signed with the Redskins in 1976.*

COACH JOE GIBBS SPEAKS WITH PRESIDENT RONALD REAGAN AFTER
WASHINGTON BEAT MIAMI 27–17 FOR ITS FIRST SUPER BOWL VICTORY.

hand, he stuck his index finger in the air: The Redskins were number one. Riggins was named the game's Most Valuable Player (MVP). "Ron [Reagan] may be president," Riggins said, "but tonight I'm king."

Washington finally had its first Super Bowl win and its first NFL title in four decades. Just as important, a new dynasty was born. The Redskins were back on top—where fans believed the team belonged. The Redskins had been one of the NFL's best teams when they started playing in Washington nearly a half century earlier.

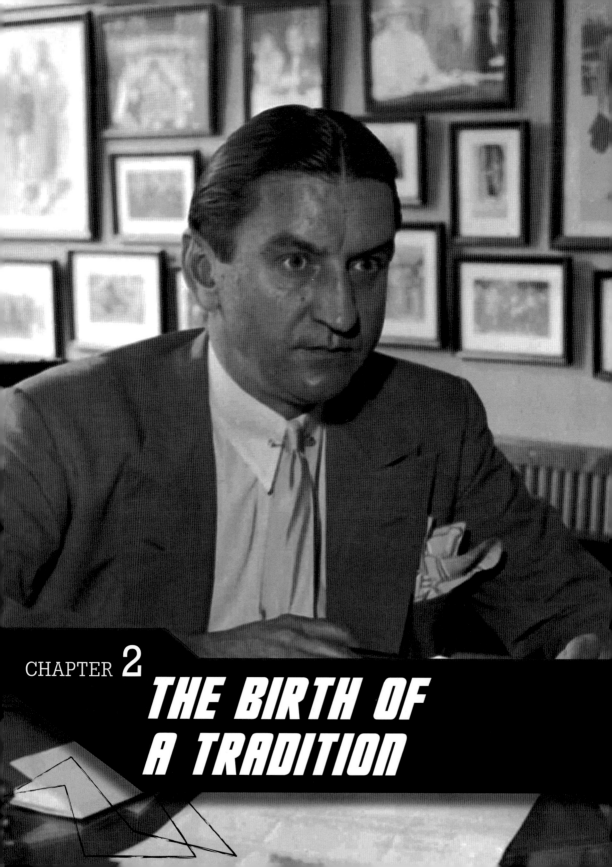

# CHAPTER 2

# THE BIRTH OF A TRADITION

**G**eorge Preston Marshall was a successful businessman in Washington DC during the Great Depression. He wanted to own a professional sports team. In 1932, the NFL wanted to add a team in Boston. Marshall was asked to buy the Boston franchise. It would be one of only eight teams in the NFL, which began in 1920.

Marshall leapt at the opportunity. The new squad would play its home games at the same stadium where the Boston Braves, a professional baseball team, played. Baseball was much more popular than football in those days. Marshall named his football team the Braves as well.

The Boston Braves went 4–4–2 in their opening season in the NFL. They then moved to Fenway Park, where the Boston Red Sox baseball team also played. Marshall wanted to keep the team's Native American link but also associate it with the Red Sox. So he changed the team's

GEORGE PRESTON MARSHALL BOUGHT THE NEW BOSTON BRAVES FRANCHISE IN 1932. IN 1936, THE TEAM WOULD CHANGE ITS NAME TO REDSKINS.

ing the team. It would play in Marshall's adopted hometown of Washington DC.

With that, the Washington Redskins were born. The decision to move paid off. The Redskins' first decade in Washington was their first golden era. From 1937 to 1945, the Redskins won two NFL crowns, played in five title games, and went 70–27–5, including playoff games.

The Redskins had one of the NFL's best players in Sammy Baugh. In that era, many players lined up on both offense and defense and sometimes kicked. Baugh stood out at quarterback, defensive back, and punter.

Baugh led the Redskins to a 7–3 start in 1937, their first season in Washington. The squad drew more than 20,000 fans in three of its six home games, a good number in the NFL at the

nickname to the Redskins. The Boston Redskins soon became one of the NFL's top squads. They reached the championship game in 1936, falling to the Green Bay Packers.

After that season, Marshall made another change. The Redskins had experienced poor attendance for much of their five years in Boston. Marshall was losing thousands of dollars. So he announced that he was mov-

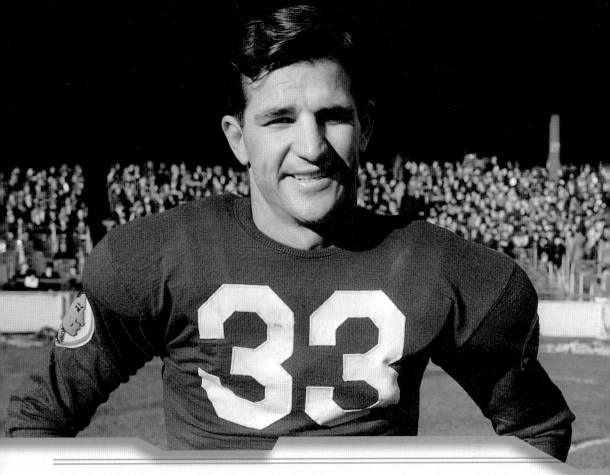

QUARTERBACK SAMMY BAUGH JOINED THE REDSKINS IN 1937. THAT YEAR, THE TEAM MOVED TO WASHINGTON DC AND WON AN NFL TITLE.

time. The Redskins' final regular-season game came on the road against the 6–2–2 New York Giants. The winner would capture the Eastern Division crown and play for the NFL title.

Washington crushed New York 49–14. A week later, the Redskins faced the Chicago Bears in the NFL Championship Game, held at Chicago's Wrigley Field. Baugh threw for 352 yards and three touchdowns as Washington won 28–21 for the team's first NFL title.

The Redskins advanced to the NFL Championship Game again after the 1940 season. But

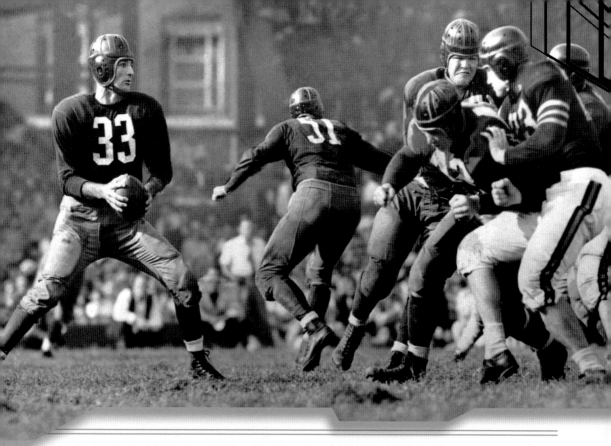

THE REDSKINS' SAMMY BAUGH LOOKS TO PASS AGAINST THE BEARS IN THE 1942 NFL CHAMPIONSHIP GAME. WASHINGTON WON 14–6.

this time the Bears routed them. Washington fell 73–0 to visiting Chicago. Through 2009, it was still the most one-sided game in NFL history. The Bears had 501 yards of offense, including 382 rushing. They intercepted eight passes, returning three for touchdowns.

In 1942, the Redskins would get their revenge on the Bears. Washington went 10–1 and

### "HAIL TO THE REDSKINS"

*George Preston Marshall started the Redskins Marching Band in 1937. He was the first NFL owner to have a team band. It is still in existence. The team song, "Hail to the Redskins," was written in 1937. Bandleader Barnee Breeskin wrote the music. Corinne Griffith, Marshall's wife, wrote the lyrics.*

won the Eastern Division. The team's opponent in the title game again was the Bears. Chicago had won 18 straight games, including the 1941 title. Baugh threw the go-ahead touchdown pass as the Redskins won 14–6. The fans at Washington's Griffith Stadium were thrilled.

Washington won the division again in 1943 and 1945. The Bears beat the Redskins to win the 1943 title, and the Cleveland Rams edged them 15–14 in the 1945 championship game.

Nevertheless, the Redskins were one of the NFL's best teams. They were confident that they would have other shots to win another league championship soon. But the franchise had to wait a long time before fielding another winning team.

## SAMMY BAUGH

Sammy Baugh excelled at quarterback, defensive back, and punter for the Redskins from 1937 to 1952. He led Washington to two NFL titles and five berths in the NFL Championship Game.

Nicknamed "Slingin' Sammy," Baugh led the NFL in passing six times. After playing at Texas Christian University, Baugh was the Redskins' top draft pick in 1937. Unlike most modern quarterbacks, he called the plays. In fact, he did not even consult with his coach.

Baugh is credited with helping transition the NFL from a run-heavy league into one that embraced the forward pass. Baugh was inducted into the Pro Football Hall of Fame in 1963.

"He was a coach on the field," said Joe Tereshinski, a Redskins wide receiver from 1947 to 1954. "He would call pass patterns and tell receivers where to go, changing them right on the field."

CHAPTER 3
# THE DOLDRUMS

**A**fter a losing season in 1963, the Redskins were aggressive in the offseason. They traded for two stars—quarterback Sonny Jurgensen and linebacker Sam Huff. They also drafted wide receiver Charley Taylor. All three would eventually be inducted into the Pro Football Hall of Fame. Yet the Redskins had a losing season in 1964 and for the next four years as well.

This is how it went for Washington for much of the late 1940s and the 1950s and the 1960s. After being one of the NFL's dominant teams for a decade, the Redskins failed to reach the postseason from 1946 to 1970.

## SONNY JURGENSEN

*Sonny Jurgensen played quarterback for the Redskins from 1964 to 1974. From 1957 to 1963, he had been with the Philadelphia Eagles. Jurgensen threw for 255 touchdowns and more than 32,000 yards in his career. Through 2009, he was eleventh in touchdowns and twenty-seventh in yards in NFL history. Jurgensen made the Pro Football Hall of Fame in 1983.*

REDSKINS QUARTERBACK SONNY JURGENSEN WALKS OFF THE FIELD IN 1967. WASHINGTON HAD PLENTY OF TALENT IN THE 1950s AND THE 1960s BUT STRUGGLED AS A TEAM.

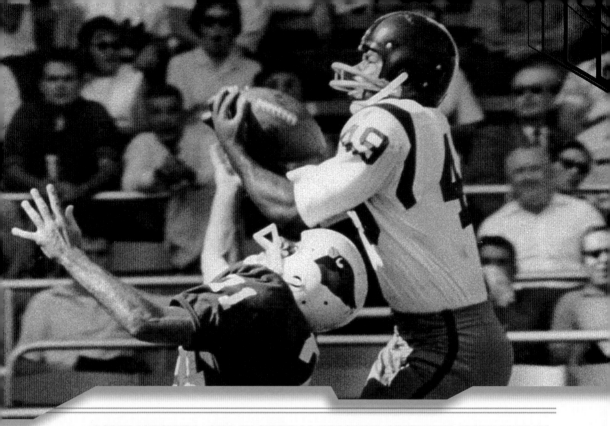

BOBBY MITCHELL, ONE OF SEVERAL REDSKINS OFFENSIVE STANDOUTS IN THE 1960s, MAKES A CATCH OVER THE CARDINALS' NORMAN BEAL IN 1962.

Washington struggled for several reasons. The franchise made bad decisions, trading away stars such as safety Paul Krause and quarterback Charlie Conerly. Washington lost players to the All-America Football Conference (AAFC), an upstart league. In addition, the Redskins failed to add a single African-American player to the roster until 1962. They were the last NFL team to employ African-Americans.

Nobody expected such a slide after 1945. The Redskins had just played in the NFL Championship Game for the sixth time in 10 seasons. But before the next season, a few players left for the AAFC and owner George Preston Marshall fired coach Dud DeGroot. Turk Edwards became coach. He led Washington to a 16–18–1 mark in three seasons.

After three straight losing seasons, Marshall let Edwards go and hired Curly Lambeau as coach in 1952. Lambeau had guided the Green Bay Packers to six NFL titles. Not even Lambeau could help the Redskins, though. They went a combined 10–13–1 in two seasons under him. He was then fired.

Marshall was blamed a lot for the losing. Besides the bad personnel moves and constant coaching changes, he also refused to add African-American players. Some historians say Marshall was racist. Others say he feared alienating Redskins fans in the South.

Regardless, Marshall gave in and the Redskins traded

## BOBBY MITCHELL

Bobby Mitchell was a halfback and wide receiver for the Redskins from 1962 to 1968. He played for the Cleveland Browns from 1958 to 1961.

Mitchell was named an All-NFL player three times. He racked up 521 career receptions and 91 touchdowns overall. Through 2009, he ranked 25th all-time in touchdowns in the NFL.

An Arkansas native, Mitchell played at the University of Illinois in Urbana-Champaign. He was inducted into the Pro Football Hall of Fame in 1983.

Mitchell was the first African-American player to join the Redskins and fought through some racism. "Bobby laid a lot of foundation," said Brig Owens, a Redskins safety from 1966 to 1977. "It took a special person to come here [as the first African-American player]. Every time they put Bobby in a position to fail, he succeeded, not just in a small way, but in a major way."

for Bobby Mitchell before the 1962 season. Mitchell was a star African-American running back with the Cleveland Browns. He quickly made the Redskins better. He had 72 catches for 1,384 yards in the 1962 season.

For the rest of the 1960s, the Redskins had a talented offense that included Mitchell, Jurgensen, Taylor, and tight end Jerry Smith. Washington's

## TEAM OF THE SOUTH

Owner George Preston Marshall grew the Redskins' fan base beyond Washington DC, staking the entire southern United States as "Redskins Country." Marshall took advantage of the fact that Washington was the NFL's southernmost city for nearly every year from 1937 to 1959, until the Dallas Cowboys were born a year later. Even in 1960 and afterward, Redskins games were broadcast to fans all over the Southeast and the team played exhibition games there. As a result, the Redskins became known as the "Team of the South." Some fans in the South still root for them to this day, even though several other NFL teams now play there.

defense in the 1960s, however, was terrible. "We had no defense," Mitchell said. "But no team had an offense that played better than us."

By the late 1960s, Marshall was ailing. Edward Bennett Williams became the Redskins' owner. In 1969, Williams outbid a few other teams to hire Vince Lombardi. Lombardi had coached the Packers to five NFL titles in the 1960s, including wins in the first two Super Bowls. He had retired to become Green Bay's general manager in 1968. But he missed coaching.

Lombardi turned around the Redskins. They started the 1969 season 4–1–1. But a late-season loss to the Los Angeles Rams helped give the Dallas Cowboys the division title. Washington finished 7–5–2 and was optimistic about its chances in 1970.

THE REDSKINS HIRED LEGENDARY COACH VINCE LOMBARDI IN 1969. HE
LED THE TEAM TO A WINNING SEASON THAT YEAR.

Then tragedy struck. During the offseason, Lombardi was diagnosed with cancer. He died during training camp. The Redskins would not recover that season. Assistant Bill Austin became interim coach. But Washington went just 6–8.

It seemed that no matter what the Redskins did, they could not become consistent winners. After the 1970 season, Williams fired Austin. Just as he did when he hired Lombardi, he turned to another veteran coach: George Allen.

CHAPTER 4 *REBIRTH*

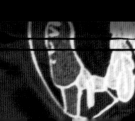

**C**harley Taylor sprinted down the sideline at RFK Stadium, past Dallas Cowboys cornerback Mark Washington, and looked up. He saw the pass from Redskins quarterback Billy Kilmer falling toward him. Taylor caught the ball in stride and raced into the end zone. Taylor's 45-yard touchdown early in the fourth quarter gave host Washington a two-touchdown lead in the 1972 NFC Championship Game.

The Redskins went on to crush the Cowboys 26–3. The win put them in their first Super Bowl. It was their crowning achievement in an era (1971–80) in which the Redskins re-emerged as an NFL power. After struggling for 25 years, they qualified for the playoffs five times in seven seasons under coach George Allen.

"George Allen put the Washington Redskins' franchise on the map," said Diron Talbert, a defensive tackle from 1971 to

THE HIRING OF FORMER RAMS COACH GEORGE ALLEN AS COACH AND GENERAL MANAGER IN 1971 HELPED TURN THE REDSKINS AROUND.

# GEORGE ALLEN

George Allen coached the Redskins from 1971 to 1977. He had coached the Rams from 1966 to 1970. He was also the general manager for Washington, which he led to an NFC title and five playoff berths.

Allen compiled a career record of 118–54–5, including playoff games, and was named NFL Coach of the Year in 1967 and 1971.

A native of Michigan, Allen was inducted into the Pro Football Hall of Fame in 2002. He was known as an innovator. Allen was the first head coach to employ a special teams coach. He also pioneered the nickel defense, using an extra defensive back on passing downs.

"He knew what it took to win," said safety Richie Petitbon, who played for Allen with the Rams and the Redskins. ". . . He started the tradition in Washington. People expect us to win. This wasn't the case in 1971."

1980. "They'd been off the map for so many years."

Allen had coached the Los Angeles Rams from 1966 to 1970. Edward Bennett Williams, the Redskins' owner, then hired Allen as coach and general manager in 1971. Allen made big changes. He traded for several former Rams, including Talbert and linebacker Jack Pardee. Allen also went with veteran Kilmer as his quarterback over the turnover-prone Sonny Jurgensen.

"The future is now," Allen declared. He was right. Washington finished just behind Dallas in the NFC East in 1971. But the Redskins earned the NFC's lone wild-card berth. They lost their playoff opener 24–20 to the 49ers at San Francisco. Yet they had enjoyed a successful season. They had finally become winners again.

THE REDSKINS' LARRY BROWN RUSHED FOR 1,216 YARDS DURING THE 1972 SEASON AND WAS SELECTED AS THE NFL'S MVP.

The Redskins had big expectations heading into 1972. Those expectations were met. The 11–3 Redskins won the NFC East title. Running back Larry Brown was named the NFL's MVP.

Washington defeated Green Bay 16–3 in the divisional round of the playoffs to set up an

## LARRY BROWN

Larry Brown played running back for the Redskins from 1969 to 1976. He was named an All-Pro twice. In his career, he rushed for 5,875 yards and 35 touchdowns and added 238 receptions for 2,485 yards and 20 touchdowns. Through 2009, Brown ranked third in franchise history in rushing yards. He amassed 1,689 combined rushing and receiving yards in 1972 in just 12 games, helping the Redskins win the NFC title.

THE REDSKINS' BILLY KILMER PASSES IN SUPER BOWL VII. WASHINGTON, PLAYING IN ITS FIRST SUPER BOWL, LOST 14–7 TO UNBEATEN MIAMI.

NFC Championship Game meeting with Dallas. It was not close. Kilmer completed 14 of 18 passes, including two that went for touchdowns to Taylor. The Redskins held the defending Super Bowl champion Cowboys to 169 yards.

The Redskins still had to play the Super Bowl, though. Two weeks later, they lost Super Bowl VII to Miami 14–7 at Los Angeles Memorial Coliseum. Kilmer threw three interceptions. The Redskins managed just 228 yards. The Dolphins finished the season 17–0. They became the first team in NFL history to complete a season unbeaten, including the playoffs.

Despite the loss to the Dolphins, the Redskins expected to

be back in the Super Bowl. Washington qualified for the playoffs again in 1973, 1974, and 1976. The Redskins went 10–4 each of those seasons. They tied for the division title twice. But there would be no more Super Bowls for Washington in the 1970s.

After the 1977 season, Allen and Williams could not agree on a new contract. Williams fired Allen and replaced him as coach with Pardee. Pardee had retired as a player six years earlier. He had coached the Chicago Bears the previous three seasons. Washington started 6–0 in 1978 but finished 8–8.

The Redskins went 10–6 in 1979. But the Bears, who had the same record, earned the final NFC wild-card berth on a tie-breaker. Washington fell apart in 1980. Running back John Riggins sat out the season in a contract dispute. Washington

finished 6–10, and Pardee was fired.

The future would bring a lot of changes. Many of the players were getting old and would have to be replaced. Williams stepped down. Jack Kent Cooke replaced him as the primary owner. Allen, University of Southern California coach John Robinson, and former Oakland Raiders coach John Madden were candidates to become the new coach. Cooke and general manager Bobby Beathard chose somebody else: little-known San Diego Chargers offensive coordinator Joe Gibbs.

CHAPTER 5
## DYNASTY

**M**ark Rypien dropped back, looked to his right, and lofted a pass toward the sideline. The ball fell into the hands of wide receiver Gary Clark. Clark ran into the end zone, extending Washington's lead in Super Bowl XXVI to 20 points over the Buffalo Bills. The Redskins would win 37–24 on January 26, 1992, at the Metrodome in Minneapolis, Minnesota.

The victory gave Washington its third Super Bowl title in 10 seasons. It was the exclamation point on an NFL dynasty.

The two main keys to the Redskins' success were excellent coaching and chemistry. "We didn't have a lot of talent, but we all knew what we had to do to win: play well together," said Art Monk, a Redskins wide receiver from 1980 to 1993.

The golden era did not start so well. Joe Gibbs lost his first

QUARTERBACK MARK RYPIEN CELEBRATES AFTER WASHINGTON DEFEATED BUFFALO 37–24 IN SUPER BOWL XXVI.

five games as Redskins coach in 1981. Gibbs and quarterback Joe Theismann settled some communication problems. Washington rebounded to finish 8–8.

Washington went 8–1 in the 1982 season, which was shortened because of a players' strike. The top-seeded Redskins beat the Detroit Lions 31–7 and the Minnesota Vikings 21–7 in the playoffs to reach the NFC Championship Game. John Riggins ran for two touchdowns and defensive tackle Darryl Grant returned an interception 10 yards for a score as Washington beat the rival Dallas Cowboys 31–17. Fans at RFK Stadium stormed the field and ripped down the goalposts.

Washington then beat the Miami Dolphins in Super Bowl XVII for its first NFL title in 40 years. Riggins provided the memorable 43-yard touchdown run in the fourth quarter.

The Redskins went 14–2 the next season and earned the NFC's No. 1 seed again. Washington edged the San Francisco 49ers 24–21 in the NFC Championship Game. The Redskins fell short of a second straight Super Bowl title two weeks later. They lost Super Bowl XVIII to the Los Angeles Raiders 38–9 in Tampa, Florida. The Raiders' Marcus Allen rushed for 191 yards and two touchdowns. The Redskins' high-powered offense could not

## JOE THEISMANN

Joe Theismann was a Redskins quarterback from 1974 to 1985. He led Washington's 1982 team to the NFL title. Theismann threw for 25,206 yards, still the most in team history through 2009. He was named the NFL's MVP in 1983, when he threw for 3,714 yards and 29 touchdowns. The Redskins traded with the Miami Dolphins for Theismann in 1974. He has worked as a football analyst on TV since retiring from the playing field.

JOHN RIGGINS DIVES FOR A 1-YARD TOUCHDOWN IN THE REDSKINS' 31–17 NFC CHAMPIONSHIP GAME WIN OVER THE COWBOYS ON JANUARY 22, 1983.

get going. Washington had set an NFL record in the regular season with 541 points.

The Redskins captured another NFC East title in 1984. But Washington lost to the Chicago Bears in the divisional round of the playoffs. The Redskins then failed to reach the

## DARRELL GREEN

*Darrell Green played cornerback for the Redskins from 1983 to 2002. He set an NFL record with an interception in 19 straight seasons. Green was named an All-Pro four times. He was inducted into the Pro Football Hall of Fame in 2008. Green was small (5 feet 8) and known for his speed. But he became a cornerback who could shut down opposing receivers by also using toughness.*

# THE HOGS

"The Hogs" was the colorful nickname for the Redskins' big, strong offensive linemen and tight ends. They dominated opposing defenses in the 1980s and the 1990s and formed the foundation for the three NFL championship teams.

Tackles Joe Jacoby and George Starke, guards Russ Grimm and Mark May, center Jeff Bostic, and tight ends Rick Walker and Don Warren were the original Hogs. Tackles Jim Lachey and Ed Simmons and guards Raleigh McKenzie and Mark Schlereth later became Hogs as well. The nickname came from offensive line coach Joe Bugel during training camp in 1982.

"I saw a lot of big, fat bellies," Bugel said. "I said, okay you Hogs. . . . It caught on." The Hogs named Bugel "Boss Hog" and made bruising running back John Riggins an honorary Hog.

postseason in 1985 despite tying for the NFC East lead at 10–6.

Heading into 1986, the Redskins had to reload after Theismann and Riggins retired. Quarterback Jay Schroeder, running back George Rogers, and Clark led Washington's offense that season. The team finished 12–4. The Redskins beat the visiting Rams in a wild-card playoff game and then traveled to Chicago. The 14–2 Bears were the defending Super Bowl champions. But Washington held star running back Walter Payton to 38 rushing yards and won 27–13. The visiting Redskins lost 17–0 to the eventual Super Bowl-champion Giants in the NFC Championship Game.

Washington finished 11–4 in a strike-shortened 1987 season and won the division. In the

DOUG WILLIAMS PASSED FOR 340 YARDS IN WASHINGTON'S 42–10 ROUT OF DENVER IN SUPER BOWL XXII ON JANUARY 31, 1988.

regular-season finale, backup Doug Williams replaced an ineffective Schroeder to rally the Redskins past the host Vikings. Gibbs announced that Williams would start in the playoffs.

The Redskins edged the host Bears 21–17 in the divisional round and held off the visiting Vikings 17–10 in the NFC Championship Game.

Cornerback Darrell Green hit Minnesota running back Darrin Nelson near the goal line in the closing seconds to break up a fourth-down pass.

Super Bowl XXII two weeks later in San Diego, California, was no contest. The Denver Broncos, led by star quarterback John Elway, were favored and took a 10–0 lead after one quarter. But Washington scored 35 points in the second quarter, a Super Bowl record. The Redskins won 42–10. Washington's Timmy Smith (204 rushing yards) and Ricky Sanders (193 receiving yards) set Super Bowl records. Williams tossed four touchdown passes and was named the game's MVP. He became the first African-American quarterback to start for a Super Bowl champion.

"In that Super Bowl, it took us a quarter to settle down, but once we did, nobody was going to beat us that day," Clark said.

The Redskins went 7–9 in 1988 and 10–6 in 1989 and did not make the playoffs either season. In 1990, the Redskins relied on running back Earnest Byner down the stretch to finish 10–6 and make the postseason. Washington beat host Philadelphia 20–6 in a wild-card game. The Redskins then lost at San Francisco in the divisional round. But Washington had returned to its roots under Gibbs: a dominant running game that opened up space for the passing game.

That is exactly how the 1991 season played out. Byner (1,048 yards), rookie Ricky Ervins (680 yards), and fullback Gerald Riggs (11 touchdowns) dominated on the ground. Rypien threw for more than 3,500 yards and 28 touchdowns.

Washington went 14–2. The Redskins beat the Atlanta Falcons 24–7 and the Detroit Lions 41–10 in the playoffs to reach the Super Bowl. Buffalo was no match in Super Bowl XXVI. Rypien, who threw for two touchdowns and 292 yards, was named the game's MVP. Riggs added two touchdowns. The defense forced five turnovers.

WIDE RECEIVER GARY CLARK RUNS WITH THE BALL AFTER MAKING A CATCH IN THE REDSKINS' 37–24 WIN OVER THE BILLS IN SUPER BOWL XXVI.

"The Redskins had one of those teams," Bills quarterback Jim Kelly said. "You almost had to play a perfect game to beat them."

The Super Bowl XXVI win is remembered as the unofficial end of an era. The Redskins were aging, and Gibbs was tiring. In 1992, Washington finished 9–7, beat Minnesota in a wild-card game, and then lost to San Francisco in the divisional round.

A few months later, Gibbs retired. He was tired. Defensive coordinator Richie Petitbon replaced Gibbs. Unfortunately for Washington, it marked the beginning of an era in which the team would struggle.

CHAPTER 6

# FRUSTRATION

**T**he Redskins' run of success from the 1981 through 1992 seasons was very enjoyable for the team and its fans. But the next 17 years were as agonizing as the previous 11 were thrilling.

After coach Joe Gibbs retired, the Redskins fell apart. The team went 4–12 in 1993. Richie Petitbon was fired as coach after the season and replaced by Norv Turner, a former Dallas assistant. Washington went a combined 9–23 in its first two seasons under Turner.

The Redskins finished 9–7 in 1996 and 8–7–1 in 1997 but missed the playoffs both times.

When Washington went 6–10 in 1998, many people thought that the team would fire Turner. Owner Jack Kent Cooke had died 1997. Daniel Snyder bought the team. But the sale was not completed until July 1999. By then it was too late to replace Turner.

The Redskins, led by newly acquired quarterback Brad Johnson, finished 10–6 in 1999. They won the NFC East title.

DANIEL SNYDER, SHOWN IN 2009, BECAME THE REDSKINS' OWNER IN 1999. THE TEAM DID NOT PLAY VERY WELL DURING HIS FIRST DECADE IN CHARGE.

Washington beat visiting Detroit 27–13 in the first round of the playoffs but then fell 14–13 to host Tampa Bay.

Despite that loss, the Redskins were excited. They were a young team with standouts in Johnson, running back Stephen Davis, and cornerback Champ Bailey. The Redskins then drafted talented offensive tackle Chris Samuels and linebacker LaVar Arrington in 2000.

The 2000 offseason, however, marked the real beginning of the Daniel Snyder era. Instead of allowing a true football expert to run the team, the young owner made many of the moves himself.

Washington began the 2000 season 6–2 but finished 8–8 and missed the playoffs. Snyder fired Turner with three games left. Coaches Marty Schottenheimer (8–8 in 2001) and Steve Spurrier

(12–20 from 2002 to 2003) were given shots to turn the team around but could not do it.

Snyder shocked nearly everyone with his next coaching hire: Gibbs. After 11 years off, Gibbs returned. The rebuilding Redskins went 6–10 in 2004. But they finished 10–6 in 2005 and qualified for the postseason. Running back Clinton Portis and wide receiver Santana Moss led the way. The Redskins beat the host Buccaneers 17–10 in the wild-card round. Washington then lost 20–10 at Seattle.

The Redskins slumped to 5–11 in 2006. Washington was

REDSKINS SAFETY SEAN TAYLOR RUNS WITH THE BALL IN OCTOBER 2007. TAYLOR DIED THE NEXT MONTH AFTER HE WAS SHOT IN A HOME ROBBERY.

5–3 at the halfway point of the 2007 season when it unraveled. Star safety Sean Taylor was injured in a loss to Philadelphia. While he was out of the lineup, thieves broke into his home in Florida and shot him. He died the next day, on November 27. The Redskins were crushed. They lost their next game, to the Buffalo Bills, to fall to 5–7.

The Washington players traveled the next day to Miami for Taylor's funeral. "We have to play for Sean," defensive tackle Cornelius Griffin said. "This is what he'd want."

# SEAN TAYLOR

Redskins safety Sean Taylor was one of the NFL's most intimidating players in his time in the league (2004–07). He grabbed 12 interceptions in his career and was named to the Pro Bowl in 2006 and 2007.

A Florida native, Taylor played at the University of Miami. He developed a reputation for delivering crushing hits to opponents and making phenomenal interceptions.

Taylor was enjoying his best season in 2007. He had five interceptions in eight games when he injured his wrist against Philadelphia on November 11. While sitting out to let the injury heal, he was staying with his fiancee in Miami. Early on November 26, thieves broke into his house and shot him. Taylor was rushed to the hospital but died the next day. Taylor's teammates and coaches attended his funeral. Several spoke. "Nobody played with more heart than Sean Taylor," running back Clinton Portis said.

Washington returned to playoff contention. With backup quarterback Todd Collins running the show, the Redskins beat the Bears, the Giants, and the Vikings. Washington was 8–7 and needed to defeat visiting Dallas for a playoff berth. The Redskins won 27–6.

The Redskins traveled to Seattle for the wild-card round and ran out of gas, falling 35–14. The next week, Gibbs said he was retiring for good.

Snyder hired former Seahawks assistant Jim Zorn as his next coach. The Redskins lost 18 of their final 24 games under Zorn. The 2009 team finished 4–12. Zorn was fired.

Late in the 2009 season, though, Snyder offered hope. He hired former Tampa Bay general manager Bruce Allen to serve in that position with

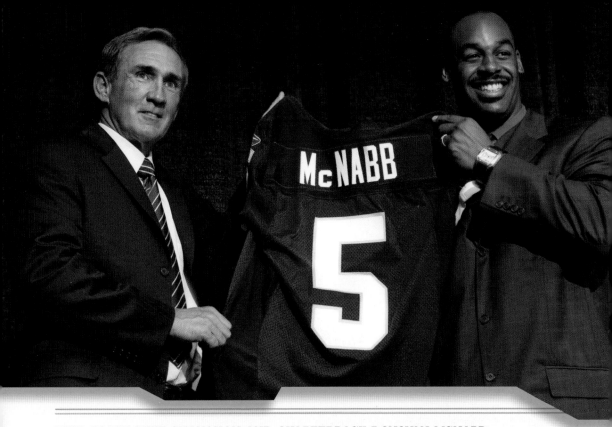

NEW COACH MIKE SHANAHAN AND QUARTERBACK DONOVAN MCNABB
POSE IN APRIL 2010 AFTER MCNABB WAS ACQUIRED FROM PHILADELPHIA.

Washington. Allen is a son of former Redskins coach George Allen. After the season, Washington hired Mike Shanahan as coach. Shanahan led Denver to Super Bowl titles after the 1997 and 1998 seasons.

To aid Shanahan, Washington acquired Philadelphia star quarterback Donovan McNabb in April 2010 for two draft picks.

On April 24, the Redskins dealt quarterback Jason Campbell, who had been the starter, to the Oakland Raiders for a draft choice. This made it clear that McNabb was being counted on to lead one of the NFL's most storied teams back to prominence.

# TIMELINE

|  |  |
|------|-------|
| **1932** | The Redskins are born as the Boston Braves. |
| **1932** | The host Braves defeat the New York Giants 14–6 on October 9 for their first win in franchise history. |
| **1937** | The club, now called the Redskins, moves to Washington. The Redskins defeat the host Chicago Bears 28–21 on December 12 to win their first NFL title. |
| **1942** | The Redskins beat the visiting Bears 14–6 on December 13 to win another NFL title. |
| **1962** | Running back Bobby Mitchell becomes the first African-American player to play for the Redskins after he is traded by the Cleveland Browns to Washington. |
| **1966** | Washington's offense hits its stride in a 72–41 home win over the Giants on November 27. |
| **1969** | The Redskins hire legendary former Green Bay Packers coach Vince Lombardi as coach. Lombardi leads Washington to a winning record. But he would die of cancer during training camp in 1970. |
| **1971** | Washington hires George Allen as coach. Allen would guide the Redskins to an NFC championship and five playoff berths in seven seasons as coach. |
| **1972** | The Redskins crush the rival Dallas Cowboys 26–3 on December 31 in the NFC Championship Game at RFK Stadium, clinching their first Super Bowl berth. |

| 1973 | The unbeaten Miami Dolphins defeat the Redskins 14–7 on January 14 in Super Bowl VII. |
|------|------|
| 1981 | Washington hires Joe Gibbs as coach. Gibbs would lead the Redskins to three NFL titles and four NFC crowns in his initial 12 seasons as coach. |
| 1983 | The Redskins defeat the Dolphins 27–17 on January 30 in Super Bowl XVII, winning their first NFL title since 1942. |
| 1984 | Washington loses 38–9 to the Los Angeles Raiders on January 22 in Super Bowl XVIII. |
| 1988 | The Redskins blast the Denver Broncos 42–10 in Super Bowl XXII on January 31. |
| 1992 | Washington tops the Buffalo Bills 37–24 in Super Bowl XXVI on January 26, winning a third NFL title in 10 seasons. |
| 1993 | Gibbs retires as coach on March 5, citing fatigue. |
| 2004 | Gibbs returns as coach after 11 years off. He would lead the Redskins to two postseason berths in four seasons. |
| 2007 | Washington beats visiting Dallas 27–6 on December 30. The win was the Redskins' fourth straight and secured a playoff spot. The team had dedicated its season to safety Sean Taylor, who was killed in a robbery in November. |
| 2010 | The Redskins hire Mike Shanahan as coach in January. In April, Washington trades two draft picks to Philadelphia for star quarterback Donovan McNabb. |

# QUICK STATS

## FRANCHISE HISTORY
Boston Braves (1932)
Boston Redskins (1933–36)
Washington Redskins (1937– )

## SUPER BOWLS
*(wins in bold)*
1972 (VII), **1982 (XVII)**, 1983
(XVIII), **1987 (XXII)**, **1991
(XXVI)**

## NFL CHAMPIONSHIP GAMES
*(1933–69; wins in bold)*
1936, **1937**, 1940, **1942**, 1943, 1945

## NFC CHAMPIONSHIP GAMES
*(since 1970 AFL-NFL merger)*
1972, 1982, 1983, 1986, 1987, 1991

## DIVISION CHAMPIONSHIPS
*(since 1970 AFL-NFL merger)*
1972, 1982, 1983, 1984, 1987, 1991,
1999

## KEY PLAYERS
*(position, seasons with team)*
Sammy Baugh (QB/DB/P, 1937–52)
Larry Brown (RB, 1969–76)
Darrell Green (CB, 1983–2002)
Russ Grimm (G, 1981–91)
Joe Jacoby (OT/G, 1981–93)
Sonny Jurgensen (QB, 1964–74)
Billy Kilmer (QB, 1971–78)
Bobby Mitchell (RB/WR, 1962–68)
Art Monk (WR, 1980–93)
John Riggins (RB; 1976–79, 1981–85)
Mark Rypien (QB, 1988–93)
Chris Samuels (OT, 2000–09)
Charley Taylor (RB/WR; 1964–75,
1977)
Joe Theismann (QB, 1974–85)
Doug Williams (QB, 1986–89)

## KEY COACHES
George Allen (1971–77):
67–30–1; 2–5 (playoffs)
Joe Gibbs (1981–92, 2004–07):
154–94–0; 17–7 (playoffs)

## HOME FIELDS
FedEx Field (1997– )
D.C. Stadium/RFK Stadium
(1961–96)
Griffith Stadium (1937–60)
Fenway Park (1932–36)

* All statistics through 2009 season

# QUOTES AND ANECDOTES

In every United States presidential election from 1936 through 2000, the result followed the result of the most recent Redskins home game. Every time the Redskins won, the incumbent party (the party that was already in office) won the election. When the Redskins lost, the incumbent party lost. That changed in 2004, when the Redskins lost to the Green Bay Packers on October 31. Two days later, George W. Bush, the incumbent Republican Party candidate, was re-elected.

RFK Stadium, where the Redskins played from 1961 to 1996, was known as one of the most intimidating places for opponents to visit. Although it seated fewer than 60,000 fans, they were close to the field and very loud. "Whenever we went into Washington, not only was the game intimidating, but the fans inside and outside the stadium were intimidating," said wide receiver Bob Hayes, a Cowboy from 1965 to 1974.

Joe Gibbs is generally regarded as the best coach in Redskins history and one of the hardest-working coaches in NFL history. "Gibbs would go out, year after year, and work 16 or more hours a day, seven days a week from July through January and sleep on his office cot four nights a week," wrote Thomas Boswell, a columnist with the *Washington Post*. "The purpose: winning football games for the Redskins and being a big success himself."

The rivalry between the Redskins and the Dallas Cowboys is one of the most intense in the NFL. "There are three great things in life: winning the lottery, having a baby, and beating the Cowboys this badly," Redskins guard Mark May said after Washington ripped Dallas 41–14 in 1986.

# GLOSSARY

### All-Pro

An award given to the top players at their positions regardless of their conference. It is a high honor as there are fewer spots on the All-Pro team than on the Pro Bowl teams.

### berth

A place, spot, or position, such as in the NFL playoffs.

### churning

Moving with vigor and purpose.

### contract

A binding agreement about, for example, years of commitment by a football player in exchange for a given salary.

### dynasty

A team that wins a lot of games, usually including more than one league championship, over a time spanning multiple seasons.

### general manager

The executive who is in charge of the team's overall operation. He or she hires and fires coaches, drafts college players, and signs free agents.

### postseason

Games played in the playoffs by the top teams after the regular-season schedule has been completed.

### Pro Bowl

A game after the regular season in which the top players from the AFC play against the top players from the NFC.

### relent

To give in; to stop being stubborn.

### wild card

Playoff berths given to the best remaining teams that did not win their respective division.

# FOR MORE INFORMATION

## Further Reading

Gehman, Jim. *Then Gibbs Said to Riggins: The Best Washington Redskins Stories Ever Told*. Chicago: Triumph Books, 2009.

Loverro, Thom. *Hail Victory: An Oral History of the Washington Redskins*. Hoboken, NJ: John Wiley & Sons, Inc., 2006.

Richman, Michael. *The Redskins Encyclopedia*. Philadelphia: Temple University Press, 2007.

## Web Links

To learn more about the Washington Redskins, visit ABDO Publishing Company online at **www.abdopublishing.com**. Web sites about the Redskins are featured on our Book Links page. These links are routinely monitored and updated to provide the most current information available.

## Places to Visit

**FedExField**
1600 Fedex Way
Landover, MD 20785
301-276-6000
www.redskins.com/gen/articles/
FedExField_524.jsp
This is where the Redskins play all their home exhibition, regular-season, and postseason games.

**Pro Football Hall of Fame**
2121 George Halas Drive Northwest
Canton, OH 44708
330-456-8207
www.profootballhof.com
This hall of fame and museum highlights the greatest players and moments in the history of the National Football League. As of 2010, 24 people affiliated with the Redskins were enshrined, including Sammy Baugh and Joe Gibbs.

**Redskins Park**
21300 Redskins Park Drive
Ashburn, VA 20147
703-726-7000
www.redskins.com/gen/articles/
Training_Camp_Frequently_Asked_
Questions_2014.jsp
This is the year-round team headquarters for the Redskins. It is where the Redskins hold their training camp each summer.

# INDEX

## About the Author

Ryan Basen is a writer and journalism professor living in Charlotte, North Carolina. A former newspaper and magazine reporter, Ryan has written books about NBA and NASCAR stars and sports issues. He earned awards from the N.C. Press Association and Associated Press Sports Editors for work he did as a reporter with the *Charlotte Observer* newspaper in 2007 and 2008.

92                                    10690
KIN           Hunter, Nigel.
              Martin Luther
        King

**DATE DUE**

| | | | |
|---|---|---|---|
| | | | |
| | | | |
| | | | |
| | | | |
| | | | |
| | | | |
| | | | |
| | | | |
| | | | |
| | | | |
| | | | |

# Martin Luther King Jr.

## Nigel Hunter

## Illustrations by Richard Hook

The Bookwright Press
New York · 1986

# Great Lives

William Shakespeare
Queen Elizabeth II
Anne Frank
Martin Luther King, Jr.

First published in the United States in 1985 by
The Bookwright Press
387 Park Avenue South
New York, NY 10016

First published in 1985 by
Wayland (Publishers) Limited
61 Western Road, Hove
East Sussex BN3 1JD, England

Second impression 1987

ISBN 0–531–18019–0
Library of Congress Catalog Card Number: 84–73575

Printed by G. Canale & C.S.p.A., Turin, Italy

# Contents

# The last great march

It was a hot day in April 1968. The streets of Atlanta, Georgia, were packed with people, and they were restless, angry, and very, very sad. They had gathered, in the city of his birth, for the funeral of Martin Luther King.

His coffin was carried on a simple farm cart, drawn by mules. Slowly, the funeral procession made its way from the family church, across town to a service at Morehouse College. Fifty thousand people joined the procession and thousands more watched it pass by. Besides his widow, Coretta, their four children, and the rest of his family, countless friends and supporters and many well-known people were there, grieving and paying tribute to a great man.

Most of the mourners were black. King had devoted his life to their freedom, and suddenly he was with them no longer. He had been murdered, shot down in cold blood. Now, it was left to others to pursue his dream.

Why was he killed? What did he do? What was his dream?

*Martin Luther King inspired a movement which gave black Americans something they had never known before – hope for the future.*

5

# Boyhood in Atlanta

Martin loved listening to his mother reading to him from the Bible.

she also played the organ at her husband's church. Martin (nicknamed "M.L.") had an older sister, Willie Christine (Chris), and a younger brother, Alfred Daniel ("A.D.") The children went so often to their father's church that they thought of it as their second home.

Ebenezer Baptist Church in Atlanta, where Martin Luther King's father was pastor.

Martin Luther King was born in 1929, in Atlanta, Georgia, in the heart of America's Deep South.

His father, Reverend ("Daddy") King, was the pastor, or minister, at Ebenezer Baptist Church, and within the local black community Martin's family was well-liked and respected. Mrs King Sr., known to Martin as "Mother Dear," was a schoolteacher and

Martin was in the church all day every Sunday, and many other afternoons and evenings too. But all the singing and shouting and joyous clapping by the congregation, praising the Lord, did not affect him as much as listening to his grandmother reading to him from the Bible.

His closest friends were the children of a local storekeeper, and young Martin enjoyed flying kites, building model planes, playing baseball in the backyard, and racing his bike with them. But he could not sit beside these friends on the bus or at the movies. Nor could they share a cool drink together at the soda fountain – or even go to the same school. Why was this? Because these friends were white, and Martin's family was black. In that part of the United States, black people and white people lived under a system of laws that forced them apart. It was known as "segregation."

*As a little boy, Martin could play with white friends in the backyard, but he could not sit beside them on a bus or at the movies. As he grew older, he could not play with them at all.*

# Segregation and the South

Segregation began after the North's victory over the South in the American Civil War of 1861–65.

Until then, for two hundred years, black people in the South had been slaves. The defeat of the Southern states ended slavery, and it was hoped that the lives of the freed slaves would improve and that black people would receive the same treatment as white people. But many white people in the Southern states still refused to treat blacks as equal citizens. They passed laws to prevent whites and blacks from mixing, and to ensure that white people remained in control.

Some whites were so violently opposed to blacks that they joined the Ku Klux Klan. This sinister organization, which terrorized and sometimes murdered blacks, had the support of some politicians and policemen.

Martin's father and grandfather were among those who had worked for justice for black people, but in all the years since the end of the Civil War, there had been little progress. Blacks were still insulted and abused throughout the South.

*Members of the Ku Klux Klan attend a ritual burning of the cross.*

# The power of words

Martin enjoyed reading, and listening to his father preach. He soon realized that words had a power that could move people to anger or to tears, to action or concern.

But words could hurt and humiliate too. One day, in a store, he accidentally stepped on a white woman's foot. She slapped his face and called him "little nigger."

Once, while riding in the family car, they were stopped by a white policeman. "Boy, show me your license," he demanded. He was speaking to Martin's father. Reverend King replied: "You see this child? That's a *boy*. I'm a *man*."

And all over the South, there were signs in public places saying "WHITES ONLY."

The Church taught a message of love, and Martin loved the Scriptures. But when it came to white people, he was unsure. "How can I love someone who hates me?" he wondered.

# Finding his way

At school Martin wanted to do well, to show that he was *someone*. His command of words dazzled teachers and classmates alike, and the rich voice that developed in his teens made him an impressive speaker.

Once, Martin went to a distant town to make a speech about the rights of black people, and he won a prize. But on the bus back to Atlanta, he was ordered to give up his seat to some white people, in accordance with the segregation laws. Martin refused to move – his prize-winning speech had attacked such laws. "You black

– – –," swore the driver, forcing the boy to leave his seat. He had to remain standing all the way home, and later said that he felt angrier then than at any other time in his life.

In the summer of 1944, when he was fifteen, Martin went to work on a farm in the North, where there were no segregation laws. He felt a great sense of freedom, visiting the restaurants and theaters in town. But returning South on the train, he was led to the back of the dining car when he went to eat, and a curtain was pulled across. Eating in the same restaurant, even on a moving train, wasn't allowed down South.

Martin went to Morehouse College, in Atlanta, to study sociology. At first he intended to become a doctor or a lawyer. But later he came to believe that he could best serve the black community as a minister. In 1947, he became his father's assistant pastor.

Left: *A refreshment shack for blacks only. Such conditions were typical in the South during the years of Martin's childhood.*

# The way forward

Martin Luther King continued his studies in Pennsylvania and at Boston University. He began to think deeply about how to achieve a more equal society for black people. He was especially influenced by the ideas of the American writer Henry Thoreau, and Gandhi, the Indian leader and social reformer.

Thoreau had written of "civil disobedience," suggesting that it could be used as a means of bringing about social change. Gandhi had put this into practice,

combining it with his own belief in the force of love. In the years of King's childhood, Gandhi had helped lead the Indian people to freedom from British rule, using "passive resistance." This meant peaceful protest by large numbers of people, who had to be willing to face armed soldiers and police. The protesters often received terrible beatings, and some were even killed.

Gandhi had encouraged the Indian people with speeches, and turned their anger into a force for good. He had taught them to think of their enemies as misguided rather than evil, and had always spoken against using violence. Finding out about Gandhi was a turning point for King. He believed that nonviolent protest was the way forward for black Americans too.

King had visited Northern cities and had seen that there, too, whites were in control. A few black people like himself were highly educated and had the

Left: *The great Indian leader, Gandhi, whose ideas had a powerful influence on King.*

promise of a glowing career, but most could hope for very little. For the millions who had to live in the ghettos – the poorest run-down areas of American cities – life could be wretched.

King was a brilliant student and he made many friends while at college. In 1953 he married Coretta Scott, who was studying music, and the following year they returned to the South.

In May 1954, he gave his first sermon as the Reverend Martin Luther King, Jr., pastor of Dexter Avenue Baptist Church in Montgomery, Alabama.

*Martin Luther King and his wife, Coretta.*

*Even in the North, black people lived in squalid, run-down areas of the cities.*

# The struggle begins

That same month, May 1954, the United States Supreme Court declared that segregated (separate) schooling was unlawful. But Southern whites refused to accept this judgement and voted that black children and white children would continue to attend separate schools for at least another year.

Meanwhile, the Dexter Church congregation was inspired by its new pastor's preaching. King was elected to a committee of the National Association for the Advancement of Colored People (N.A.A.C.P.), which battled in the courts on behalf of black people.

Now, across the Southern states, the Ku Klux Klan began a campaign of terror. A young black boy named Emmett Till was murdered by a white mob, who, hearing a rumor that he had whistled at a white woman, dumped him in a river with barbed wire and machine parts around his neck. And they went unpunished.

The insults and injuries seemed never ending. Day by day, black people's anger grew. What could unite them in their struggle for equal rights?

On the Montgomery buses, black passengers were continually insulted by the drivers, who were all white. They were prevented from using the front seats or sitting next to white passengers, and they had to give way for whites who wanted to sit. Sometimes, after paying a fare at the front, a black passenger was told to get off and go to the door at the back – and the bus would roar away before there was time to step on again.

*A meeting of the Ku Klux Klan.*

Many drivers tended to treat black women especially badly. But on December 1, 1955, Rosa Parks, a middle-aged seamstress who worked for the Montgomery N.A.A.C.P., tired after a long working day, refused to give up her seat to the white man who was demanding it. No, she would *not* budge. The police were called, Mrs Parks was arrested – and the battle against the bus laws began.

*Old racist resentments came to the surface in Birmingham, Alabama.*

15

# Boycott the buses!

The black people of Montgomery decided it was time to make their feelings clear. They decided to boycott (refuse to use) the buses. Then the city leaders would have to take notice. So, within a few days, there were no black passengers on the buses. Everybody was walking, hitchhiking or bicycling instead.

King was elected president of a new black pressure group and he addressed thousands of supporters. "We are tired of being segregated and humiliated, tired of being kicked about. If we are wrong, justice is a lie," he declared. He led a group of protesters to talk to the Montgomery city authorities, asking for equal treatment on the buses. Their demands were refused, so the boycott went on.

The black people of Montgomery formed car pools, sharing their cars to help each other with transportation, although many preferred to keep on walking, protesting "with their feet."

King received messages of support from people all over the United States, from whites as well as blacks. But some people accused the boycott's leaders of being "unAmerican," and sent them threatening letters. King often feared for his life and for his family's safety, but he decided he had to continue his work despite the risks. He believed that God was telling him to fight on.

Then his house was bombed. Fortunately no one was hurt – but no one was arrested for the outrage. Later King was tried and found guilty of breaking a local law against boycotts, but he was released when the case went to a higher court. Martin Luther King and the bus boycott had become internationally famous, and he toured the country making speeches.

For months, the protest continued. Then, at last, the U.S. Supreme Court declared that Alabama's bus laws were "unconstitutional" (against the country's guiding principles). This meant that the buses would have to be de-segregated. And so, with determination, and the leadership of Martin Luther King, black Americans had won their first great victory.

*The black people of Montgomery walked, hitchhiked and even rode mules, rather than use the buses.*

# Leading the struggle

*The faces of the white students show their anger as black students attempt to enter Little Rock High School.*

protest and began to treat the city's blacks with respect. Others, however, resented their success: black churches were bombed, and again King's house was attacked. But finally the terror stopped, and King could begin planning for the future.

In March 1957, King went to Ghana in West Africa, to attend that country's independence celebrations. Africa impressed him deeply and he compared the struggle of black Americans with freedom movements all over the world.

The success of the Montgomery bus boycott encouraged black people throughout the South, and new protest groups were formed in many cities. The black people's churches were at the heart of the movement for social change and Dr. King was soon regarded as a natural leader in the struggle for civil rights.

Many whites in Montgomery recognized the success of the bus

# Slow progress

In 1957, Congress met to consider changing the laws so they would better protect black people's rights. Thirty-five thousand people made a "Prayer Pilgrimage for Freedom," gathering in Washington to support the call for a change in the laws. They sang out loudly, calling for voting rights and for equal rights in housing and education. King and other black leaders met Vice President Nixon, asking him to take action to improve the rights of American blacks.

Changes in the law were made – but not enough. In September a court ordered that nine black students could attend the Central High School at Little Rock, Arkansas. The first black student to try to enter the school was Elizabeth Eckford. She was driven back by crowds of jeering whites, and soldiers too. This was a challenge to the law, and after weeks of ugly scenes which shocked many Americans, President Eisenhower was forced to send in other troops. For the following months, the students could only go to school with the protection of these troops.

# "We shall overcome"

King was disappointed by a meeting with President Eisenhower who, it seemed, would do little to speed up changes in the laws.

In September 1958, King was arrested and violently beaten. The police had not recognized him. He said at his trial, "America is in danger of losing her soul." He was found guilty of loitering, and would have gone to prison, but the Police Commissioner paid his fine, calling the affair a "publicity stunt."

A few weeks later King was stabbed and seriously wounded while in New York. After

*President John F. Kennedy.*

recovering, he traveled to India. Seeing Gandhi's homeland, and remembering what peaceful protest had achieved there, he felt encouraged in his own work, and returned home renewed in spirit.

Early in 1960, students in the Southern states began demanding equal rights for blacks and whites at restaurants and cafeterias. They held sit-in protests, and the words of the soon-to-be-famous protest song *We Shall Overcome* rang out across the lunch counters. Many whites, and many police, reacted with violence, but the students kept the protests going. King, urging nonviolence, joined them at a snack bar, and again he was arrested and imprisoned.

This time there was powerful

*Student demonstrators sit-in, campaigning for desegregation of restaurants and lunch counters.*

help from Senator John F. Kennedy, soon to be president. The arrested protesters were released, but not King. He was given four months' hard labor, in connection with an earlier traffic violation. Finally, with Kennedy's help, he was freed. Lunch counter segregation was abolished in many southern cities.

In May 1961, groups of blacks and whites together, called Freedom Riders, set out to protest about segregation in Southern bus stations. The Klan attacked them violently while the police stood by. At one point, hundreds of frenzied whites surrounded a church where King was speaking. Fearing it would be destroyed, King desperately telephoned the White House. Fortunately, Federal troops were already on the way to help. John F. Kennedy had recently been elected, and at last, it seemed, there was a president who cared.

*The police looked on while, inside the church, King and his congregation were threatened by frenzied white mobs.*

# The "nonviolent army"

*In his cell King wrote his famous* Letter from Birmingham Jail.

King now devoted himself wholly to the civil rights cause. Across the South the protest movement grew: many campaigns were successful, and it often seemed that black people were making real progress. But some campaigns failed, and a number of protesters even lost their lives.

The city of Birmingham, Alabama, was, said King, the most segregated city in the country. In 1963, the civil rights campaign there became international news. People all around the world could see on their television screens what black Americans were up against. They saw the police dragging protesters away from marches and sit-ins. The Police Chief, "Bull" Connor, had ordered his men to "jail 'em all," and said he was dedicated to "keeping the niggers in their place."

King was arrested and put in a cell. This time he accepted prison as a "badge of honor." In his cell King wrote a letter defending the actions of the protesters. He wrote that a law which uplifts us is just, and one that degrades us is unjust

– and that it is right to disobey unjust laws. *The Letter from Birmingham Jail* was smuggled out and has been honored as a classic statement of "civil disobedience," ever since.

After a week, King was released, and at this point, thousands of children joined the protest against segregation in Birmingham. The police used their dogs, and high-pressure fire-hoses, to drive the protesters back. Men, women and children rushed to the safety of their churches, but many people were badly hurt in the chaos.

Day after day, the demonstrations and brutality continued. Police filled the prisons with people, arresting as many as fifteen hundred schoolchildren, some no more than six years old.

King with his young son, in front of his house, where the Ku Klux Klan had left its symbol – a burned cross.

A mounted sheriff's posse chases civil rights demonstrators in Montgomery.

# The dream of Martin Luther King

*King, with his wife Coretta, leads a march for civil rights.*

All over the world people watched what was happening in Birmingham on TV news programs. President Kennedy was deeply concerned, and ashamed at this picture of America. He persuaded the Birmingham city authorities to accept some of the protesters' demands. But a thousand Ku Klux Klansmen rallied together, and there were violent clashes between whites and blacks before desegregation at last began to take place.

At the end of August 1963, there was a great march on Washington, the nation's capital. A quarter of a million people, both black and white, called powerfully and passionately for civil rights for black Americans. At the rally they heard Martin Luther King's most famous and inspiring speech, in which he talked of his dream:

> I have a dream that my four little children will one day be judged, not by the color of their skin but by the content of their character. I have a dream today. I have a dream that one day little black boys and black girls will be able to join hands with little white boys and white girls and walk together as sisters and brothers. I have a *dream* today.

Martin Luther King's speech came from the heart, and all the people who heard him were greatly moved.

But back in Birmingham, two weeks later, the violence returned. Denise McNair, who was eleven, and her friends Addie Mae Collins, Carol Robertson and Cynthia Wesley, who were all fourteen, were killed by a bomb. It exploded as they were preparing to sing in the church choir.

*King's stirring speeches, and his constant insistence on nonviolence, inspired and moved his audiences, wherever he spoke.*

And then, on November 22, 1963, the dreadful news came from Dallas, Texas: President Kennedy was dead too, assassinated as he drove through the city. "This nation is sick," said King. "I don't think I can survive either."

# Enemies at home – honor abroad

King had made many enemies over the years, including the powerful boss of the F.B.I., J. Edgar Hoover. Hoover insisted that King and other black leaders were communists, and the F.B.I. often "bugged" King's hotel rooms with secret microphones, hoping to trap him in scandal. There were also rivals to King within the black movement itself. One was Malcolm X, a leader of the Black Muslims, who disagreed with King's nonviolent methods.

But, in striving for justice and always rejecting violence, Martin Luther King was honored throughout the entire world. Towards the end of 1964, he was awarded the Nobel Peace Prize. Proudly, he traveled to Norway to accept it at the grand awards

ceremony. In his speech he looked forward to "the bright daylight of peace and brotherhood" that would follow "the starless midnight of racism and war." And he praised the courage of all who took part and suffered in the movement for civil rights.

Having preached, too, at St Paul's Cathedral in London, King returned home to a hero's welcome.

*In Oslo, he is congratulated after receiving the Nobel Peace prize.*

# The right to vote

Congress passed a Civil Rights Act in 1964, as a tribute to John F. Kennedy. This ensured further desegregation, but, as before, few blacks in the South were accepted as voters.

In 1965, in Selma, Alabama, a great campaign for black voting rights took place. Thousands of marchers of all ages, including many hundreds of white people, took part. The demonstrations were met with ferocity by state troops, and scenes as bad as those in Birmingham once again outraged the world. King called on white church leaders to join the protests, and after one of them was clubbed to death, President Johnson made a speech to Congress. "The time for waiting is gone," he said. He proposed a bill that would guarantee voting rights to all Americans.

King led a spectacular march from Selma to Montgomery. Twenty-five thousand people, white and black, met at the state capital. They sang "we shall overcome." Five months later the Voting Rights Bill became law.

# Conflict in the cities

In other parts of the country, discontent among black Americans was growing too. In the ghettos, peaceful protest had not worked. Housing was bad, unemployment high, wages low, and police brutality all too common. Before long, American cities, from coast to coast, were being torn by riots, and "Black Power" became the rallying call.

In the conflict of the Vietnam War, blacks were dying in the name of freedoms they were denied at home. King became deeply involved in the anti-war protests that swept the nation. He believed the war was a disaster and a national disgrace, an unjust war which suggested that America was "a society gone mad."

He felt that the money being spent on the war should, instead, be used to help America's poor. He planned a campaign of civil disobedience in Washington for the spring of 1968. There, the nation's poorest citizens, whites as well as blacks, would attempt to change government policies. But it was not to be.

# "The Promised Land"

In April 1968, King went to Memphis, Tennessee, to support the black workers in an industrial dispute. During the past months, the number of threats to his life had been increasing. "It doesn't matter to me now," he said in a speech on April 3rd. "I've seen the promised land. I may not get there with you, but we as a people *will* get to the promised land."

Within twenty-four hours Martin Luther King was dead – shot down by James Earl Ray.

King died at the age of thirty-nine. How much more he might have achieved, we can only wonder. As it is, his life gave great strength and purpose to black Americans. Even today, problems remain – but for many, the quality of life has improved greatly. To other people too, all over the world, King gave belief in the power of peaceful protest to change the future. Protest marches and acts of "civil disobedience" are an essential part of the worldwide peace movement today.

On April 4, 1968, shock and despair, rage and bitter grief touched people everywhere. But the name, the deeds, the *dream* of Martin Luther King – these at least can never fade.

*"I may not get there with you, but we as a people* will *get to the promised land."*

# Important dates

1929   January 15: Martin Luther King born in Atlanta, Georgia.
1944   Enters Morehouse College, Atlanta.
1947   Ordained: becomes assistant pastor at Ebenezer Baptist Church.
1948   Graduates from Morehouse with degree in Sociology.
      Enters Crozer Seminary, near Philadelphia, Pennsylvania.
1951   Graduates from Crozer with degree in Divinity: top of his class.
      Enters Boston University for Ph.D. in Theology.
1953   Marries Coretta Scott.
1954   Becomes pastor of Dexter Avenue Baptist Church in Montgomery, Alabama.
1955   Awarded Ph.D.
      Works with the Montgomery N.A.A.C.P.
1956   Leads Montgomery bus boycott.
1957   Travels to Africa and Europe. Prayer Pilgrimage to Washington. Civil Rights Act.
1958   Works with the Southern Christian Leadership Conference in a Crusade for Citizenship.
1959   Travels to India. Resigns Dexter Avenue pastorship.
1960   Lunch counter protests.
1961   Freedom Rides.
1963   Anti-segregation protests in Birmingham, Alabama.
      Washington March: King's speech, "I have a dream . . ."
      Assassination of President John F. Kennedy.
1964   Civil Rights Act. Awarded Nobel Prize for Peace.
1965   Demonstrations in Selma, Alabama, for black voting rights.
      Assassination of Malcolm X. Large-scale riots begin in the North as well as the South. President signs Voting Rights Act, August 6.
1966   Moves to Chicago, Illinois, to work against poverty in the ghettos.
1967   Speaks out against the war in Vietnam.
1968   April 4: Assassinated in Memphis, Tennessee.

# New words

**Black Power**   The slogan of blacks who sought economic and political power beyond civil rights.

**Boycott**   To refuse to use – in this case the Montgomery buses.

**Civil disobedience**   Deliberate illegal action, aimed at getting "unjust" laws changed.

**Civil rights**   Rights due to all citizens – to vote, to receive equal treatment under the law, etc.

**Congregation**   A group of people gathered for worship in a church.

**Deep South**   The southeast part of the United States, especially the states of South Carolina, Georgia, Alabama, Mississippi and Louisiana, which were the heart of slavery in the U.S. before the Civil War.

**Desegregate**   To end racial segregation.

**F.B.I.**   The Federal Bureau of Investigation. A government agency responsible for investigating crimes against the State.

**Ghetto**   The crowded slum area of a city, where members of a socially-deprived minority live.

**Ku Klux Klan**   A secret organization of white Protestant Americans, mainly in the South, who use violence against blacks and other minority groups.

**Loitering**   Standing about aimlessly – in law, with a view to committing a crime.

**N.A.A.C.P.**   The National Association for the Advancement of Colored People. It aims for complete equality before the law for black Americans.

**Nobel Prizes**   Awards made every year for achievements in science, economics, literature and peace. They are considered to be the world's highest honor.

**Passive resistance**   Nonviolent resistance by such means as fasting, peaceful demonstration, and noncooperation.

**Posse**   A group of men who assist a sheriff to keep law and order.

**Racism**   Aggressive attitude by members of one race towards another.

**Segregation**   A system of laws and customs which aim to separate white people from black people.

**Supreme Court**   The highest court of law in the United States.

# Books to read

Bains, Rae. **Martin Luther King**. Mahwah, NJ: Troll Associates, 1985.

Harris, Jacqueline L. **Martin Luther King, Jr.** New York: Franklin Watts, 1983.

McKissack, Patricia. **Martin Luther King, Jr.: A Man to Remember.** Chicago, IL: Childrens Press, 1984.

Millender, Dharathula. **Young Man With a Dream**. New York: Bobbs-Merrill, 1983.

# Index